My Gardening Journal

garden specifications

What is the character of your garden? Is it small or large,
hilly or flat, shady or sunny? Are there acres of grass, or is it
largely paved? What type of soil does it have? Use this space to
record your garden's specifications and special features.

notes on projects and designs

Mango Languages - Russian
Greetings Gratithdes and Goodbyes

Strastwetзвä'a - Hello to stranger formal/Be healthy *anytime of day*
Dobree↑   - Good /literally kind
Dean   - Day
Vi'atcha   - Evening
Utrra   - Morning   Dobrra Utrra
Breeviet   - Hi informal
Goc   - How
vagh̃   - are your   vash -formal
Di̇͠a↗   - things

estimated budget

item or service

what it will cost

item or service	what it will cost

item or service

what it will cost

item or service

what it will cost

notes on shrubs and trees

shrubs and trees planting record

name of shrub or tree	where & when it was planted, & comments

name of shrub or tree   where & when it was planted, & comments

31

name of shrub or tree   where & when it was planted, & comments

name of shrub or tree   where & when it was planted, & comments

name of shrub or tree   where & when it was planted, & comments

God Almighty first planted a garden; and, indeed, it is the purest of human pleasures.
FRANCIS BACON, *Essays 46, 'Of Gardens'*.

notes on perennials

name of perennial   where & when it was planted, & comments

name of perennial   where & when it was planted, & comments

name of perennial

where & when it was planted, & comments

name of perennial

where & when it was planted, & comments

name of perennial   where & when it was planted, & comments

name of perennial   where & when it was planted, & comments

name of perennial   where & when it was planted, & comments

notes on annuals

name of annual   where & when it was planted, & comments

48

name of annual

where & when it was planted, & comments

name of annual   where & when it was planted, & comments

name of annual

where & when it was planted, & comments

name of annual   where & when it was planted, & comments

name of annual

where & when it was planted, & comments

notes on bulbs

name of bulb   where & when it was planted, & comments

name of bulb   where & when it was planted, & comments

name of bulb

where & when it was planted, & comments

name of bulb

where & when it was planted, & comments

notes on herbs

Fino & research purslane

name of herb

where & when it was planted, & comments

name of herb   where & when it was planted, & comments name of herb

where & when it was planted, & comments

notes on vegetables

name of vegetable   where & when it was planted, & comments

name of vegetable	where & when it was planted, & comments

name of vegetable

where & when it was planted, & comments

name of vegetable   where & when it was planted, & comments

notes on fruit

name of fruit   where & when it was planted, & comments

name of fruit   where & when it was planted, & comments

name of fruit | where & when it was planted, & comments

name of fruit

where & when it was planted, & comments

spring

Put up Pickles from Monica's cucumbers Aug 9, wednesday
Check on the 12th around 6 Pm

summer

fall

winter

A gardener's work is never at an end.
JOHN EVELYN, *Kalendarium Hortense.*

inspirational notes

resources

The Alpine Garden Society
AGS Centre
Avon Bank
Pershore
Worcestershire WR10 3JP
UK
+44-(0)1386 554790
www.alpinegardensociety.org
Encourages interest in alpine and rock garden plants, including bulbs, ferns, and hardy orchids.

American Horticultural Society
7931 East Boulevard Drive
Alexandria, VA 22308
USA
+1-703-768-5700
www.ahs.org
Offers gardening and horticultural education for all skill levels, and information on any garden subject.

The Garden History Society
70 Cowcross Street
London EC1M 6EJ
UK
+44-(0)20-7608-2409
www.gardenhistorysociety.org
Aims to promote the study of garden history and garden conservation.

The Herb Society
Sulgrave Manor
PO Box 946
Northampton NN3 0BN
UK
+44-(0)845-491-8699
www.herbsociety.org.uk
Aims to increase the understanding, use and appreciation of herbs and their benefits to health.

The Herb Society of America
9019 Kirtland Chardon Road
Kirtland, OH 44094
USA
+1-440-256-0514
www.herbsociety.org
Promotes knowledge, use and enjoyment of herbs through research and educational programmes.

National Gardening Association
1100 Dorset St.
South Burlington, VT 05403
USA
+1-802-863-5251
www.garden.org
Aims to help and inspire gardeners of all levels of skill and experience.

The Hardy Plant Society
Little Orchard
Great Comberton
Pershore
Worcestershire WR10 3DP
UK
+44-(0)1386-710317
www.hardy-plant.org.uk
Aims to stimulate interest in growing hardy herbaceous plants.

The National Garden Scheme
Hatchlands Park
East Clandon
Guildford
Surrey GU4 7RT
UK
+44-(0)1483-211535
www.ngs.org.uk
Publishers of *Gardens of England and Wales Open for Charity*, also known as the Yellow Book.

The Royal Horticultural Society
80 Vincent Square
London SW1P 2PE
UK
+44-(0)845-260-5000
www.rhs.org.uk
Organizes the Chelsea Flower show. Four open gardens around the UK.

The Society of Garden Designers
Katepwa House
Ashfield Park Avenue
Ross-on-Wye
Herefordshire HR9 5AX
UK
+44-(0)1865-301523
www.society-of-garden-designers.co.uk
Affiliated to the RHS.

nurseries and suppliers

name	tel
address	fax
	e-mail
	www

name	tel
address	fax
	e-mail
	www

name	tel
address	fax
	e-mail
	www

name	tel
address	fax
	e-mail
	www

name	tel
address	fax
	e-mail
	www

name	tel
address	fax
	e-mail
	www

name	tel
address	fax
	e-mail
	www

name	tel
address	fax
	e-mail
	www

nurseries and suppliers

name	tel
address	fax
	e-mail
	www

name	tel
address	fax
	e-mail
	www

name	tel
address	fax
	e-mail
	www

name	tel
address	fax
	e-mail
	www

name	tel
address	fax
	e-mail
	www

name	tel
address	fax
	e-mail
	www

name	tel
address	fax
	e-mail
	www

name	tel
address	fax
	e-mail
	www

nurseries and suppliers

name   tel

address   fax

e-mail

www

name   tel

address   fax

e-mail

www

name   tel

address   fax

e-mail

www

name   tel

address   fax

e-mail

www

name   tel

address   fax

e-mail

www

name   tel

address   fax

e-mail

www

name   tel

address   fax

e-mail

www

name   tel

address   fax

e-mail

www

nurseries and suppliers

name		tel
address		fax
		e-mail
		www

name		tel
address		fax
		e-mail
		www

name		tel
address		fax
		e-mail
		www

name		tel
address		fax
		e-mail
		www

name		tel
address		fax
		e-mail
		www

name		tel
address		fax
		e-mail
		www

name		tel
address		fax
		e-mail
		www

name		tel
address		fax
		e-mail
		www

nurseries and suppliers

name	tel
address	fax
	e-mail
	www

name	tel
address	fax
	e-mail
	www

name	tel
address	fax
	e-mail
	www

name	tel
address	fax
	e-mail
	www

name	tel
address	fax
	e-mail
	www

name	tel
address	fax
	e-mail
	www

name	tel
address	fax
	e-mail
	www

name	tel
address	fax
	e-mail
	www

nurseries and suppliers

name _____ tel _____

address _____ fax _____

_____ e-mail _____

_____ www _____

name _____ tel _____

address _____ fax _____

_____ e-mail _____

_____ www _____

name _____ tel _____

address _____ fax _____

_____ e-mail _____

_____ www _____

name _____ tel _____

address _____ fax _____

_____ e-mail _____

_____ www _____

name _____ tel _____

address _____ fax _____

_____ e-mail _____

_____ www _____

name _____ tel _____

address _____ fax _____

_____ e-mail _____

_____ www _____

name _____ tel _____

address _____ fax _____

_____ e-mail _____

_____ www _____

name _____ tel _____

address _____ fax _____

_____ e-mail _____

_____ www _____

book list

book list

First published in the United Kingdom in 2002
This edition published 2011
by Ryland Peters & Small
20–21 Jockey's Fields
London WC1R 4BW

and in the USA
by Ryland Peters & Small, Inc.,
519 Broadway
5th Floor
New York, NY 10012

www.rylandpeters.com

10 9 8 7 6 5 4 3 2 1

ISBN 978 1 84975 089 9

Printed and bound in China.

Text & design © Ryland Peters & Small 2002, 2011

Illustrations Pages 8, 11, 31, 35, 39, 40, 48, 53,
59, 67, 70, 73, 77, 88, 95, 96, 101, 106, 143 & 144
© Ryland Peters & Small. Reproduced from *Creating
Boundaries & Screens* and *The Kitchen Garden*, both
by Richard Bird; *Gardening with Herbs* by George
Carter; and *Spring in the Garden* and *Summer in the
Garden*, both by Steven Bradley.

Photographs Cover photograph by Pia Tryde,
page 13 Jerry Harpur, pages 2 & 110 Andrea Jones,
page 102 James Merrell, & page 54 Francesca Yorke
all © Ryland Peters & Small.
All other photographs © Steve Painter.